PERFIDIOUS

Written and illustrated by Mauro Marchesi

Collins

1. THE GREATEST THIEF IN THE WORLD

Is everything looking OK?
Yup. Everything's running smoothly.
Our museum has the best safety devices.
Not even Perfidious will get in.
I'm more worried about the schoolchildren visiting the exhibition tomorrow!
WO WO WO WO WO WO WO
??

It's the alarm in the Hittite artefacts hall!
PERFIDIOUS!!!
Good evening, gentlemen.
Shut the doors! *HURRY!*
LARM
CLIK
SBAM
PRIVATE
WLAM

The steel doors are a nice touch ...
F-freeze!!
Reinforcements are on their way!
I can get out the way I came in.
Anthrony? Activate the winch.
WIIIR
Right away, Sir.
Adios amigos!
SWIIIISSSSS
Woah!
Activate the new security grid!

BRAND NEW
LASER
GRID ®
CLIK
SIZZLE

Why wasn't I aware of this new laser security grid, Anthrony?
I'm afraid my database hasn't fully updated.
You're trapped!
Outstanding move, officer. Congratulations.
Not as long as I have my Stink-O-Jelly® spray.
SLOSH
FSSSSS
HA!

FSSSSSSSSSS
I can create a wall around me with this gel!
It will interrupt the grid and I can safely pass through.
Bleah!
Umph!
Awful, isn't it? The smell's not necessary ... but it makes everything more fun.
SGWISH
Now I'm going to show you another little invention of mine.
THUGS
As soon as the capsules come into contact with air they expand!
POP POP POP POP POP POP POP POP POP POP

Each one transforms into a faithful and hardworking helper:
THE THUGS!
VLAM
Stop! This time I've got you!
You're too late, Inspector Hound.
Anthrony, prepare the pigeons.
Of course, Sir.
GET TO THE ROOF! STOP HIM!

The pigeon slippers are activated and ready to fly.
WOOOIIINNG
The Thugs will dissolve in an hour so the police can't study my secret technology.
Thanks, Anthrony. Are we on schedule?
Everything as planned.
I'll get you! You hear me?
I WILL GET YOU!
Good night, Inspector! See you soon!

Trentbourg district, 00:15 a.m.
I'm in the sewers. Disable the safety systems in tunnel 23.
Infrared, lasers and cryogenic inhibitors off.
Activating voice command to open the doors.
DANGER DO NOT CROSS TUNNEL 23
Pizza rules!
CLIK!

SWIIIIIIIIISH
Welcome back, Sir. Congratulations on the masterfully executed job.
Thanks, Anthrony. Update me on the parental situation.
They're enjoying ice cream in the living room.
Good.
Prepare the ladder for the undressing.

Ahh ... my sweet secret lair.
MHUSK
MOBILE HUSK
CLAK!
FSSSSSS
TLACK
Uh-oh ... code red, Sir.

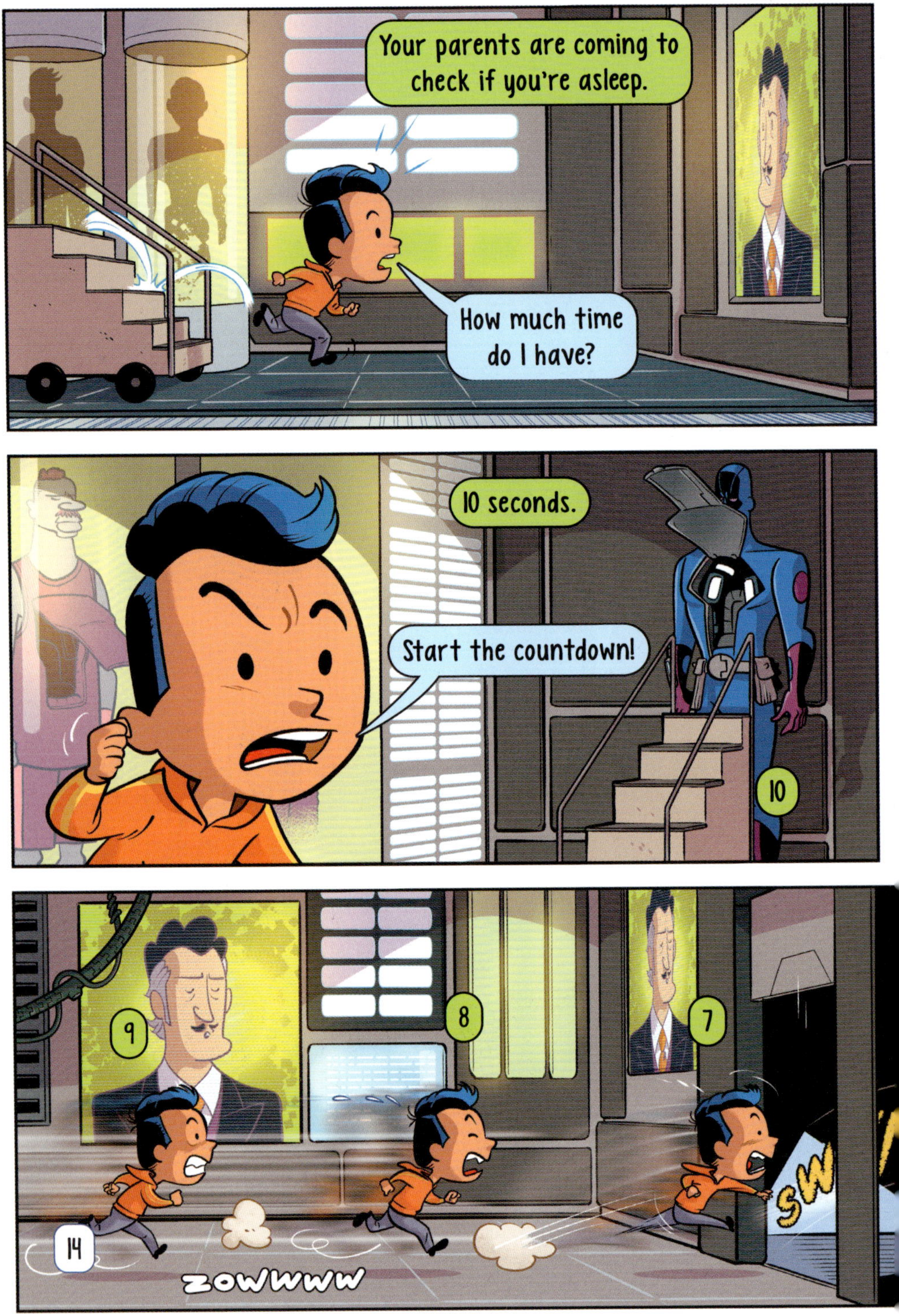
Your parents are coming to check if you're asleep.
How much time do I have?
10 seconds.
Start the countdown!
10
9
8
7
ZOWWWW

2
ZOMP
3
TUP
4
5
6
SKREE
CLUK!
1
Contact.
Shhh.
CLICK
He's sleeping like an angel.

The next day . . .
Good morning, class. Unfortunately, the Guggenstein Museum is closed due to a break-in last night.
ELEMENTARY SCHOOL WILL B. KLEVER
Too bad, I loved Paul's visit proposal.
Oh no ...
So there's no educational trip, Miss Petula?
Of course there is, Mirna. We're going with Ramal's suggestion – a visit to the Video games world fair.
C D E
YEEEEEESS
AH AH AH AH AH AH AH AH AH AH AH AH
Success!

2. I KNOW WHAT I LIKE

What a fake.
Mind your own business, Paul.
OK. Be as quick as possible.
I'll be quick!
What's up, Ramal?
Hi Vinod, I don't feel well.
Then you're in luck. It's veggie soup for lunch. It will do you a ton of good.
Yucky soup! Not if I can help it ...

CLAK
Eh eh ...
K-KREEEEK
... my little safety net, just in case ...
BLIP
And now, let's get down to business.
RUN
RUN
RUN

CLANK
Rafa Maintenance Service
ZOO
SWISS
Time for a quick disguise!
TUD
GNIEK
VRRRRRRR
Anthrony, do you copy?
Loud and clear.
VROAAMMMM

WRRRRR
City Hall
Did you upload my ID into the city database?
Of course.
Good morning.
Good morning. How can I help?
I'm here to inspect the air conditioning.
One moment, please, while I check your details.
TICK TICK TACK

Rafa Maintenance Service.
That's me.
Here's your pass. You'll need the basement.
Thanks, I know where that is.
Have a good day.
I will.
Take the corridor to the right. Then first door on the left.
Use the swipe card.
SWIP
BEEEP
You have 15 minutes.
That's plenty of time, Anthrony.
CREAAK

OK, Anthrony.
I'm looking at the street map of Grandville.
I'm uploading the virus through the system.
Fourteen minutes to go.

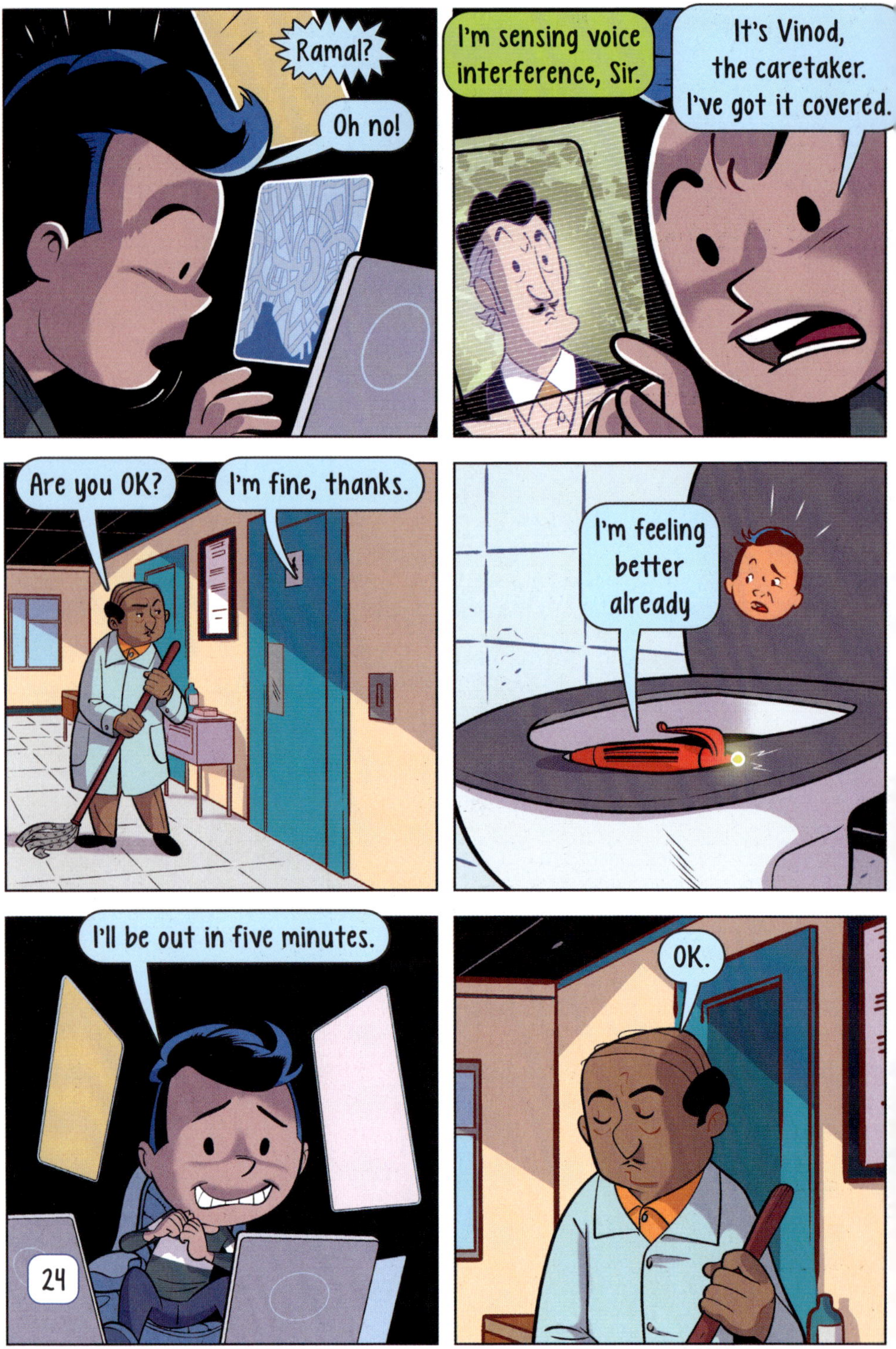
Ramal?
Oh no!
I'm sensing voice interference, Sir.
It's Vinod, the caretaker. I've got it covered.
Are you OK?
I'm fine, thanks.
I'm feeling better already
I'll be out in five minutes.
OK.

POIT
SWOIIIIIING
FLASH
Yes!
FA-FLASH
Success!

Now that's a traffic jam!
Very clever indeed, Sir.
BEEEEEEEPP
HOONK
BLARE
BEEEPP
BEEEEP
HOOOONNK

Time's up. The technicians are coming ...
Time to go!
Green light – no pun intended – ha ha!
What's going on?
I don't know.
The traffic control system has gone haywire.
All done!
Why didn't you hack the system remotely?
Because this way is more perfidious!

Hi Vinod.
Hey, Ramal.
I'm going back to class now.
Make it quick. Your teacher will think you've got lost.

Later ...
RIIIIIIIIINNG
OK class, it's lunch time.
Don't run! Enjoy your meal.
I love "veggie Thursday". The soup is delicious!
Mmm – yes.

Hi Ramal, are you feeling better?
Much better. I'm starving!
Then you're in for a treat.
The catering truck delivering the veggie soup is stuck in the biggest traffic jam ever seen in Grandville.
So it's pizza instead.
Yes!
I hate veggie soup.
BEEEP
BEEP
HONK
SCHOOL CATERING
HOOGA
BLARE

3. THE HOUSE OF CARDS

I'll be back to base in 15 minutes, Anthrony.
All right, Sir, your dinner is waiting.
WEEEEEEE
Get him, Sergeant O'Hara!
He's ours, Inspector Hound.

Grandville police station.
I wonder where he's going?
Maybe he's working on his next heist, Chief.
Or maybe he's returning to his hideout.
Setting up a surveillance team with these new Hoversuits® is proving to be successful, Inspector Hound.
It's the best technology we have.

Radar reports flying objects behind you.
Yes, I saw them, Anthrony.
It's Inspector Hound's latest attempt to catch me.
What about the disengagement plan?
WEEEEEE
I was thinking about option 15B.
Excellent choice.
I'll be home in 20 minutes. Keep my dinner warm.

BLIP
Activate hologram!
GRUUUUUUUUUUUUU
Ahhh ... Sergeant! It's an enormous capybara!
WEEEEEEEE
Take evasive action!

SBAM
ZOW
We've ended up in a rubbish pile. Perfidious tricked us with ... a giant capybara hologram.
AHAHAH
Sergeant O'Hara! What's happened?
ARRRHHH! He fooled me again!
WEEEEEEEEEE

The next morning, outside Will B. Klever Elementary School.
Is he coming?
Did he say he was actually bringing it?
Yes. Paul always keeps his word.
ELEMENTARY SCHOOL WILL B. KLEVER
That's him! That's him!
Hi Paul. Did you bring it?
Come on, show it to us.
I've got it right here in this protective case.

The limited-edition card of Vigamor 4 from Technotronik Chronicles®!
WOW
So that's the limited-edition card.
Yes, of course it is.
It's very hard to find, but my father owns Spectacular Trading Cards Ltd.
You can write an article in the school paper, Mirna, and interview me!
Maybe ...

Paul's been boasting about that card all week!
The night before ...
I'm in, Anthrony ...
Roger that.
SPECTACULAR
TRADING CARDS LTD
The rare cards produced by Spectacular are stored on the lower floor.
You need armoured box 5B.
LOCKER 5B
TC LIMITED EDITION
I'm going to cut the glass.

ZZZZZZZZZZZZZZzz
Perfect Anthrony. I have the printing plates for the limited edition Vigamor 4 card.

Get the printing machine ready, Anthrony.
How many copies do you want to print?
Let's start with 10,000!
Radar reports flying objects behind you.
Yes, I saw them, Anthrony.
Those officers in flying suits were never going to catch me!

There are only three copies of this card. It's very rare and valuable.
I'm sure you'll want a picture for the school paper.
Er, not really, Paul.
Hey Paul, can I hold it?
Only I can hold it the right way.
It's very, very valuable.
Hey, look up there! It's a drone!
What?

WWWUUUUUZZZZ
Look, it's dropping pieces of paper on the school!!!
YEEH
But ... Wait! They seem ...
It's the limited-edition Vigamor 4 card!

YEEH
WAHHH
There are thousands of them ...
10,052 to be precise.
Mysterious drone drops limited-edition cards on the school.
Now that's an interesting story!
Sigh ...

I feel a bit sorry for Paul.
I wonder who was operating the drone?
Who knows? Probably an extremely cool guy.

Ramal's guide to being Perfidious

4. Use cutting-edge technology.
5. Fool the police!
WEEEEEEEEEE
6. Always have an escape plan.

Ideas for reading

Written by Gill Matthews
Primary Literacy Consultant

Reading objectives:

- read books that are structured in different ways and reading for a range of purposes
- use dictionaries to check the meaning of words that they have read
- check that the text makes sense to them, discuss their understanding and explaining the meaning of words in context
- draw inferences such as inferring characters' feelings, thoughts and motives from their actions, and justifying inferences with evidence

Spoken language objectives:

- articulate and justify answers, arguments and opinions
- maintain attention and participate actively in collaborative conversations, staying on topic and initiating and responding to comments
- participate in discussions, presentations, performances, role play, improvisations and debates

Curriculum links: Relationships education – Respectful relationships

Interest words: austere, sensational, caper, identity

Build a context for reading

- Ask children to look at the front cover of the book and describe what they can see. Ask who or what they think Perfidious is. Support them in looking up the meaning of *perfidious* (deceitful).
- Look at the back cover. Ask children to predict the kind of events that might happen in the story. Discuss how knowing what perfidious means might help them to understand what type of character he is.
- Point out that this is a graphic novel. Explore children's knowledge and experience of graphic novels. If necessary, explain that in a graphic novel the story is told through both words and pictures.

Understand and apply reading strategies

- Ask children to turn to pp2–3 and to decide in which order the frames should be read. Focus on the first frame on p3 and ask in which order the speech bubbles should be read.